This publication is protected under the US Copyright Act of 1976 and all other applicable international, federal, state and local laws, and all rights are reserved. Please do not distribute this book in any way. Please do not sell it, or reprint any part of it without written consent from the author. Except for the inclusion of quotation, always include a link to the author's site: valeriethedoula.com.

This publication is based on personal experience and anecdotal evidence. The author assumes no responsibility for errors or omissions. This guide is not intended to replace common sense, legal, medical or other professional advice, and is meant to inform and entertain the reader. All scripture verses of the Bible taken from biblegateway.com in multiple versions including New Living Translation, New International Version and New King James.

Initial designs by Monica Gibbs. The Drawing Tree, LLC.

Some original photos by Paul Anthony Reed

Copyright © 2014: Valerie Lenon-Reed, "Valerie The Doula" and Raising Little Humans. All rights reserved worldwide.

I'm Praying For You Baby

Scripture Inspiration
For Speaking Life
Over Your Child
Starting In The Womb

This book is dedicated to all MOMS —You were chosen by God for this privileged journey. Soak in every moment from the first positive test to the first sound of the heartbeat to the moment your deliver your little human into this life. Cherish your gift(s) and don't doubt for a second that you were made for this.

BE ENCOURAGED

A mother's prayers have amazing power. You are your child's first prayer warrior. Hit the battlefield for your child today. Begin now and then never cease to pray for them. It is never too early to start praying for your baby. Yes, when born they are brand new but the issues of life have not changed. So, now is the time to start speaking life over every experience your child will have in his or her lifetime. Your prayers starting when your baby is in the womb have more than an impact than you'll ever realize. Prayer not only sets a peaceful and comforting tone for your pregnancy, it ignites something in the spirit that you and your baby will share in together. Through prayer, you invite God's love and power into every moment of your pregnancy from your anxiety and worry to your expectations and joy. It doesn't matter if you've ever had the habit of praying prior to pregnancy. This book chronicles the prayers and scripture affirmations a mother can pray as she journeys through the beauty of the life growing inside.

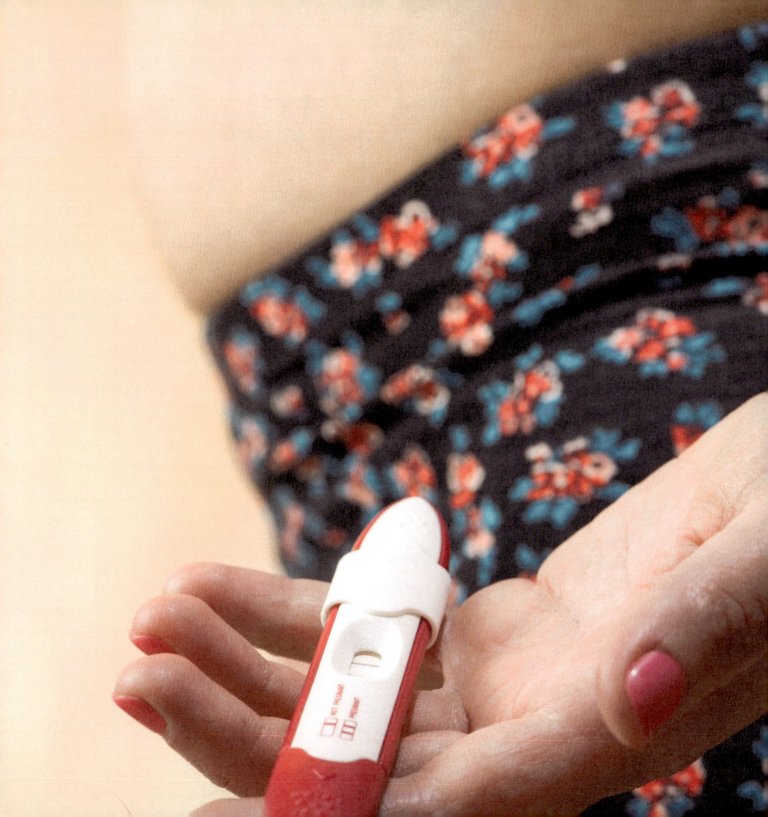

1 CORINTHIANS 13:13

"And now these three remain; faith, hope and love. But the greatest of these is love." THANK YOU GOD for LOVING ME. Father God, thank you for allowing me to experience love in this LIFETIME. Thank you for your Son, Jesus; my Savior. Because you love me God, I BELIEVE that ANYTHING is POSSIBLE. I thank you Father for this child born from your love and into love. I BELIEVE that because you are love, I am love and my child is love. I declare in Jesus' name that my child is LOVING. I pray for the WISDOM to share your love and Jesus' commandment to love, with my baby. I declare that your love is the FOUNDATION of my household. Teach me to show love in everything I do as a mother and as I raise my child. CHANGE ME to be the example of your love that my child needs to see. I thank you God in advance that my child will SPREAD YOUR LOVE throughout their experience here. I declare Father God that this baby will take to HEART your kind of love and SHARE it with others. I pray that my baby always knows that YOUR LOVE is the REMEDY and CURE for everything in life.

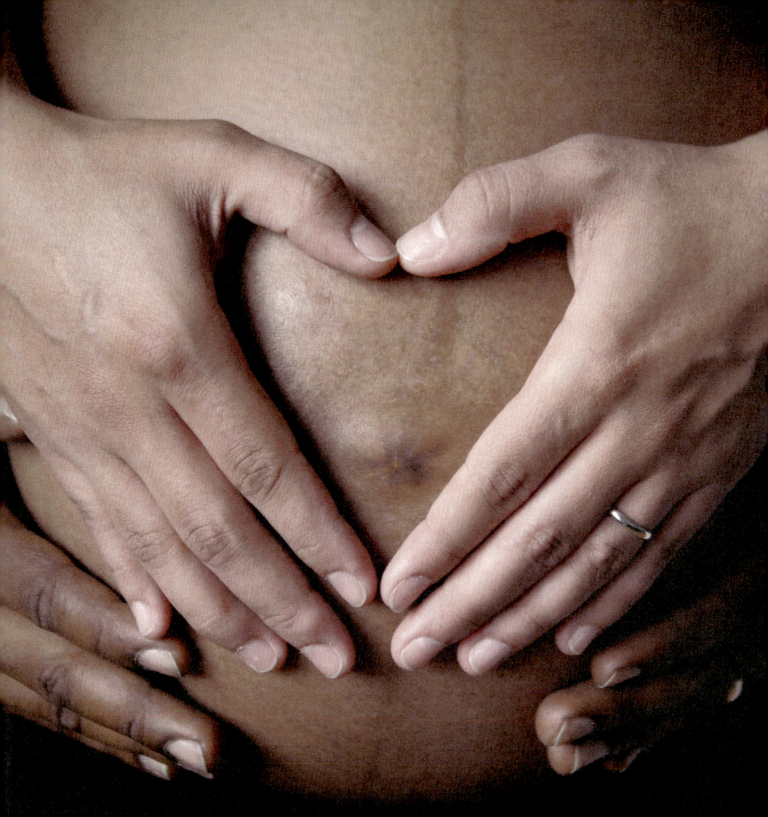

MATTHEW 18:4

"So anyone who becomes as humble as this little child is the greatest in the kingdom of heaven." Lord God I pray that my child will be a HUMBLE, self-less, KIND, PATIENT, forgiving and gracious person. I pray Father God that my baby will PRAY humbly, live MODESTLY and you will allow PROMOTION to bless and reward their humility. I pray my child has an attitude of OBEDIENCE, SUBMISSION and they possess the WILLINGNESS to put others first. I declare Father God that in all situations; my child's attitude will be that of BLESSING others with GRACE, MERCY, RESPECT and FORGIVENESS. I pray that my child is happy to allow others to shine and win. I pray God that my child will humbly admit their needs, shortcomings and humbly come before you when they require WISDOM. I declare that my child is not prideful but humbly receives advice and happily PRAISES and builds up others. God, I pray that my child grows to have a selfless HEART, willful submission to YOUR BEST and being used for your GLORY.

PSALM 127:3

"Behold, children are a heritage from the Lord, the fruit of the womb a reward." I praise you Father God that you chose to BLESS me with the tremendous GIFT of being a MOTHER. Because you have entrusted me with this SPECIAL role in life, I pray for my baby in every way including the HEALTH of my body as I feed my baby and my SPIRIT. Thank you that my baby's total WELL-BEING is secure because of your FAITHFULNESS to your WORD. I pray Father God that your angels surround my baby's labor and delivery fulfilling YOUR WILL for their BIRTH into this life. I pray that your hand be on the doctors and nurses assisting with this MIRACLE. Reveal to me Father God, how I should prepare for this new season. Show me how to be the best mother for my child. I ask that your GRACE to be an ANOINTED MOTHER for this child while providing them with whatever they need on their JOURNEY to fulfilling YOUR PLAN and PURPOSE for their life.

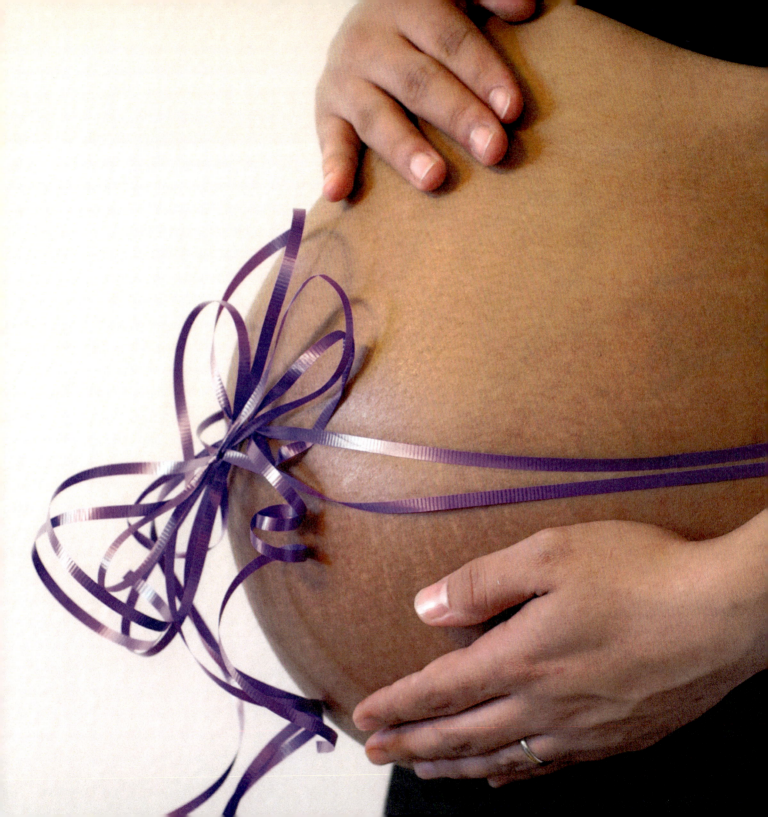

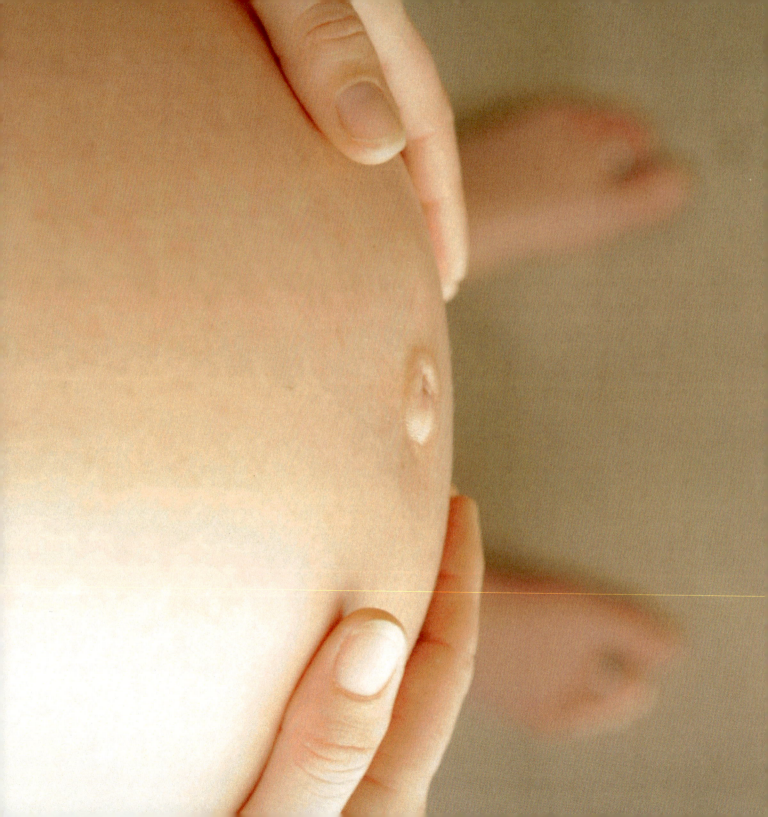

1 JOHN 4:16

"We know how much God loves us, and we have put our trust in his love. God is love, and all who live in love live in God, and God lives in them." God, I pray that my child **CHOOSES YOU**. I pray that my child comes to know **YOUR LOVE** for themselves. I pray God that your love **OVERWHELMS** my child in every area, shadow, path and season of their life. Father God, I pray that your love will **TRANSFORM** and mold as they journey towards **FULFILLING YOUR PERFECT WILL**. I pray that my baby continually develops a **HEART** that is **OPEN** and **WILLING** to all that you'll need to do in and through them. God I pray that my child learns to **RELY ON YOUR LOVE**, as their **ONLY SOURCE**. God I pray that because your love is so **POWERFUL** in their life, my child will be **GENTLE** and **KINDHEARTED** in all relationships and will learn to be **LOVING, MERCIFUL, TENDER** and **COMPASSIONATE** towards everyone. I declare in Jesus' name that my child will always show **YOUR LOVE**.

HEBREWS 12:1

"Therefore, since we are surrounded by such a huge crowd of witnesses to the life of faith, let us strip off every weight that slows us down, especially the sin that so easily trips us up. And let us run with endurance the race God has set before us." God, I pray my child grows to have a STRONG MIND. I pray that my child finds STRENGTH in living for you and accomplishing the plan you have for their life. Lord God, teach my child PERSEVERANCE and help them develop DISCIPLINE so that they see through to completion all that you've called them to ACHIEVE for your glory. I declare that my child is a GOOD WORKER who is COMMITTED and DILIGENT. God, I ask that you bless the work of my child's hands. I pray that they experience SATISFACTION and FULFILLMENT because they achieve their goals. I pray Father that they seek you for STRENGTH, FOCUS and CLARITY and anything else that they need because they know that YOU ARE their SOURCE. I declare that because they MOTIVATED and DETERMINED to please you, they will be RICH, WEALTHY and FULL according to YOUR WORD.

ISAIAH 54:13

"All your children will be taught by the LORD, and great will be their peace." I thank you Father God, that your **WORD** ignites so much **PEACE** in my life. Lord God, you are my **PERFECT PEACE** and I speak your peace over my baby. I pray that your Word is the foundation of my baby's life. I pray that my baby learns that **YOU ARE EVERYTHING** they will ever need and so they will rest no matter what's going on around them. I declare that my child **WORSHIPS** you and **HONORS** you. Thank you in advance Lord God that your **SUPERNATURAL** peace **RESTS, DWELLS** and **RULES** over my child's life. I pray that my child experiences everything that adds to their peace; **WHOLENESS, COMPLETENESS,** nothing lacking; nothing lost. I declare that your peace guides them and keeps them **CALM** and **CONTENT**. I pray that my child makes all decisions after first consulting you and acts when they have your peace in their heart. God, I thank you that my child is a **PEACEFUL** person. I declare that my child is a **PEACEMAKER** and it is their heart's desire to choose peace in all circumstances.

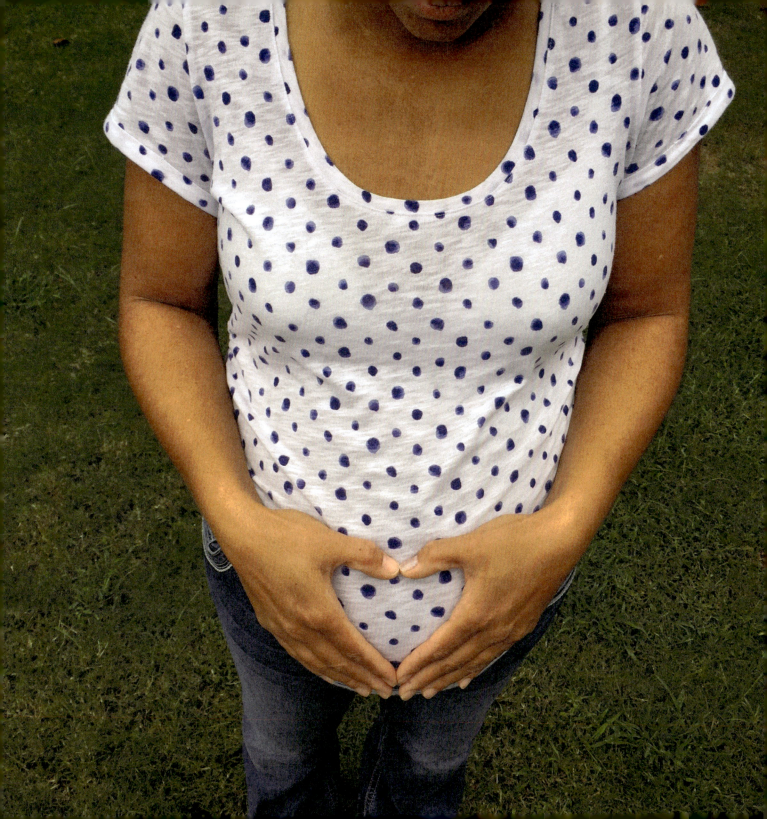

PSALM 25:21

"May integrity and honesty protect me, for I put my hope in you." God, I pray that my child grows to be an HONEST person. I pray God that you will instill in my baby a love for the TRUTH. I pray that they speak the truth in all situations no matter what. I pray that my child settles for no less than the truth in their relationships, fellowships and business. God, I pray God asking you to fill my child with COURAGE to stand for the truth without wavering. I pray Father that my child is CONFIDENT when speaking the truth and I pray that they find courage in knowing you will PROTECT and HONOR them for their FAITHFULNESS to doing what is right. I pray Father, that because my child endeavors to be TRUTHFUL, that they will attract truth to their experiences. I pray God that my child is consistently someone who can be TRUSTED and I pray that they develop a REPUTATION for being a person of INTEGRITY. I pray God that my child's truth INSPIRES others to live lives of integrity as well.

 BOY?

 girl?

1 JOHN 5:4

"For everyone born of God overcomes the world. This is the victory that has overcome the world, even our faith." I declare in Jesus' name that my child is **VICTORIOUS**! In advance, I declare in Jesus' name that my baby has won every single victory, **OVERCOME** every challenge and defeated every obstacle that they will ever face. I declare that they will win and that their victory will be **FAIR**. I thank you Father God that my baby will live a life of **VICTORY** and **WINNING** according to your will. In Jesus' name, I declare that my child **WINS** and **PROSPERS** in all things that please you, Father God. I pray God that my child knows that their victory was bought and paid for by Jesus Christ and their victory is **ALREADY WON**. God, I pray that my child will live a life of courage and expect the best because they believe in your love, Word and **PROMISES**. I pray that my child will experience many personal **VICTORIES** and they will have **TESTIMONIES** that **ENCOURAGE** others towards faith in you.

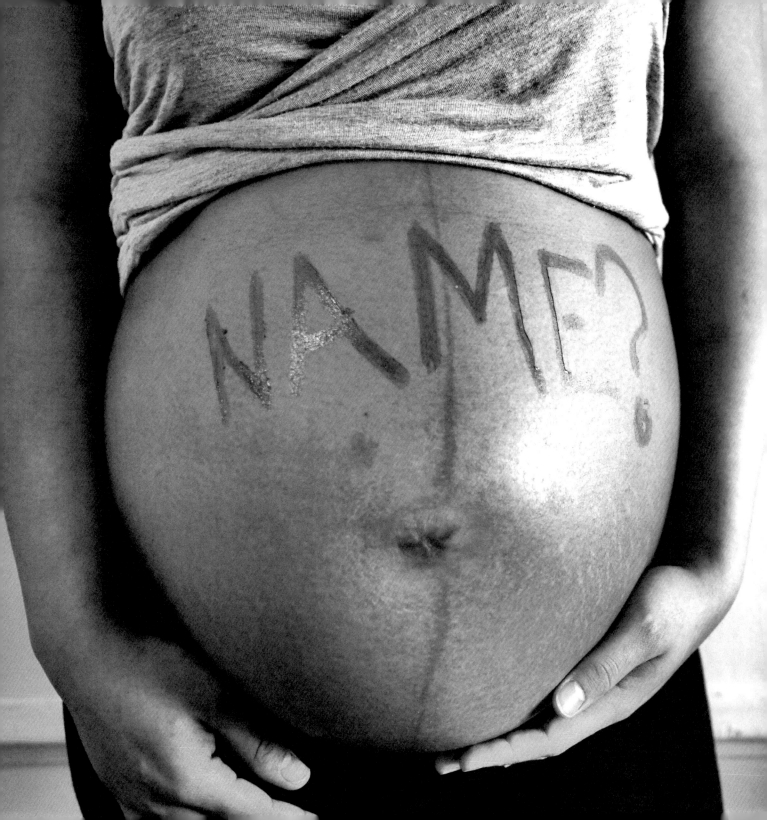

ROMANS 12:2

"Don't copy the behavior and customs of this world, but let God transform you into a new person by changing the way you think. Then you will learn to know God's will for you, which is good and pleasing and perfect." I declare that my child is a LEADER. I declare in Jesus' name that my child is EXCITED to follow the example of Christ. Lord God, I pray that my child will live their life as UNIQUELY as you created them to be; UNASHAMED of all the little and huge details of their personality and character. I pray God that my child will seek you to understand their CALLING, GIFTS and TALENTS. I pray that my child will use their talents only to HONOR and GLORIFY you. I pray Father God that peer pressure will not affect my child's life and that they will OVERCOME all temptations. I pray Lord that they will not conform to any INFLUENCE of this world but will have DIVINE CONNECTIONS who will be good influences and POSITIVE support. I pray God that my child will have a decisive mind that's focused on living life YOUR WAY.

EXODUS 15:2

"The Lord is my strength and my song; he has given me victory. This is my God, and I will praise him— my father's God, and I will exalt him!" Lord God, I pray that my baby has a HEART that wants to sing YOUR PRAISES and WORSHIP YOUR GOODNESS. I declare in Jesus' name that my child is a LIVING TESTIMONY all the days of their life. I pray that when others see my child, they see you Father God. Lord, I pray that my baby will grow to experience ENJOYMENT and HAPPINESS every time they think of how awesome you are. I declare that no matter what comes their way, my child will know that BREAKTHROUGH can be found in their praise of YOUR AWESOMENESS and power. I pray that my child finds REJUVENATION, RESTORATION, ENERGY whenever they sing about your love. I pray that whether in the BRIGHTEST or darkest hour, my child will LIFT UP YOUR Holy NAME and receive your FAVOR. I pray God that because of their praise and worship, my child inspires others to accept Jesus Christ and follow you.

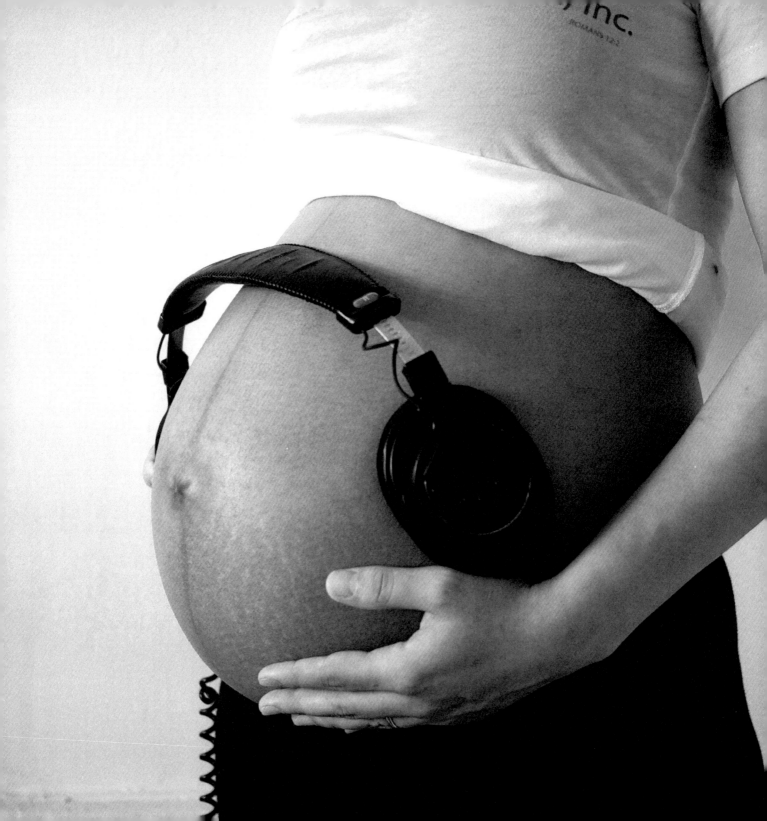

3 JOHN 1:4

"I could have no greater joy than to hear that my children are following the truth." My precious baby, I pray that GOD and HIS WORD become everything to you! I pray that you go to God's Word for your every need, question, curiosity, RESOLUTION, SOLUTION and COMFORT. God, I pray that the TRUTH of your Word is my baby's only source of WISDOM and LOVE in all the situations they will encounter in this life. Lord, I pray that my child develops a HUNGER for your Word. I pray that my baby will seek KNOWLEDGE and GUIDANCE only from you. I declare in Jesus' name that my child will gain JOY, SATISFACTION and FULLNESS from reading and SPENDING TIME with your Word and accepting your PROMISES for their life. I pray that my baby will CONFIDENTLY TRUST your Word and will seek you first and seek your Word as FIRST and FINAL AUTHORITY. I declare in Jesus' name that the Word is the truth that will guide my child through to VICTORY.

2 CORINTHIANS 5:7

"For we live by believing and not by seeing." I pray that my baby will LIVE A LIFE OF FAITH. I pray God that my child will protect their faith with their life and that they won't allow anything to decrease or threaten their faith in you. I ask Father God that you SPEAK to MY CHILD'S HEART and INCREASE their FAITH when they have needs or when fears and worries arise in their life. I pray that because of your love for them, their faith will GROW STRONGER and stronger. I declare that my child will live a life of FULLNESS because of their unwavering faith in you. I pray that because of their faith in you, your Word and YOUR PROMISES, my child's faith will be their CENTER and GUIDING LIGHT. I pray God that my baby will continually grow SPIRITUALLY STRONG and decisive. Father God, I pray that my child will be a STRONG WITNESS for Jesus Christ because of their faith in you as their everything. I declare in Jesus' name that my child will INSPIRE others with their life of faith and their LIVING TESTIMONY.

PROVERBS 18:10

"The name of the lord is a strong fortress; the godly run to him and are safe." Lord God, I pray that your **ANGELS ENCAMP** around my baby keeping them from hurt, harm and danger all the days of their life. I pray Father God that my child is **SAFE**. I pray that my child is safe in all environments and around all people. I pray that **GREAT IS THE PEACE** of the community and every person that my child encounters. I pray God that at all times, **YOUR PRESENCE** will surround and **SHIELD** my child and dissolve all their fears. I pray that whenever my baby calls on your name any time throughout their life, they will **BE CONFIDENT** that you are their **STRONG FORTRESS** within whom they will find **PROTECTION**. I pray Father God asking that you **PROTECT** my child from all threats of the enemy. I **PLEAD THE BLOOD OF JESUS'** over my child's life and I declare that they are safe from the enemy's attack on their peace. Thank you God for your faithfulness.

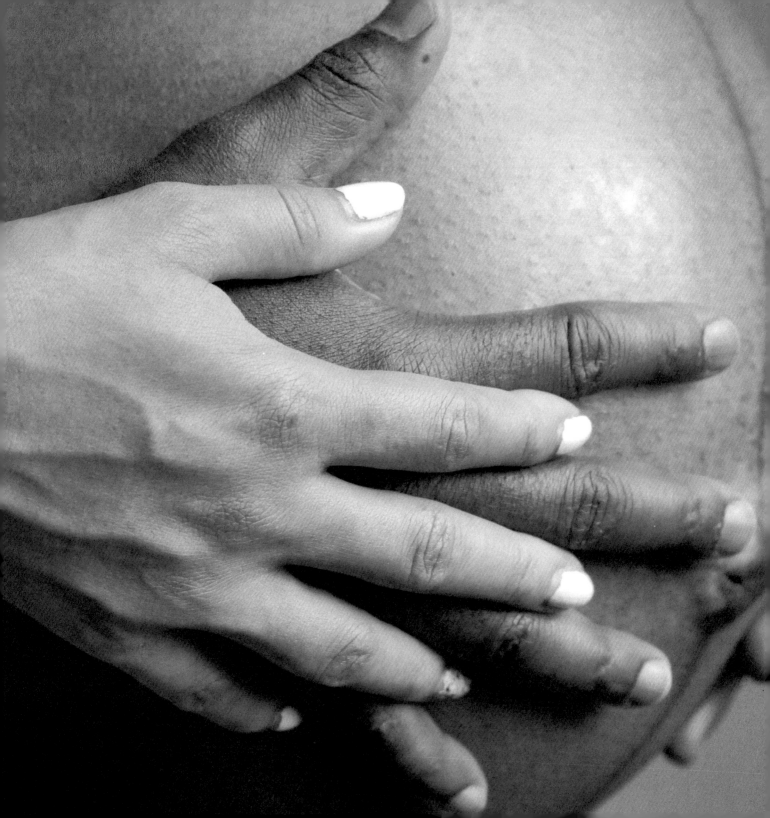

EPHESIANS 6:18

"And pray in the Spirit on all occasions with all kinds of prayers and requests. With this in mind, be alert and always keep on praying for all the saints." I declare in Jesus' name that my baby will become a **PRAYER WARRIOR**! God, I ask that you create in my baby a strong **SPIRITUAL HUNGER** to communicate with you and for **PRAYER LIFE** that will **SUSTAIN** and strengthen them throughout life. Father God, I pray that my child **YEARNS** to communicate with you and accepts prayer as a **PRIVILEGE**. I pray God that my child will understand that prayer is their **POWER** and that in all circumstances they can pray and be **CONFIDENT** that you will hear them and answer. I declare that my child **BOLDLY** and confidently brings their every thought before you God because they trust in your love. **STRENGTHEN** and **NOURISH** my child through their prayers, Father. God, I pray that my child will develop a **HEART** that **PRAYS FOR OTHERS**. I pray that my child can be trusted to be a **COMMITTED** and **SINCERE** prayer warrior for their sister or brother in need of faith.

PSALM 139:13

"For you created my inmost being; you knit me together in my mother's womb." I thank you God for your love. I thank you Father God your Word says that you have created us with an awesomely unique plan for our lives. So, God I declare in Jesus' name that my child will ACCOMPLISH the AMAZING plan that you have for their life. I pray God asking you to reveal to my child their purpose so that daily they live CONFIDENTLY and COURAGEOUSLY for you. Speak to them Father God regarding their gifts and talents. I pray that everything they need, they will SEEK and find only in you. Lord, where they are weak, make them STRONG. God, where they need HELP for the journey, be there with them EVERY STEP of the way. Lord I pray that your Holy Spirit will lead them in the way they should go. I pray God that their life HONORS YOU and brings you joy. I pray my child PROSPERS in their mind, body soul and spirit according to your intricate design. And Lord, I pray that nothing stops or hinders my child from becoming all that you've created them to be.

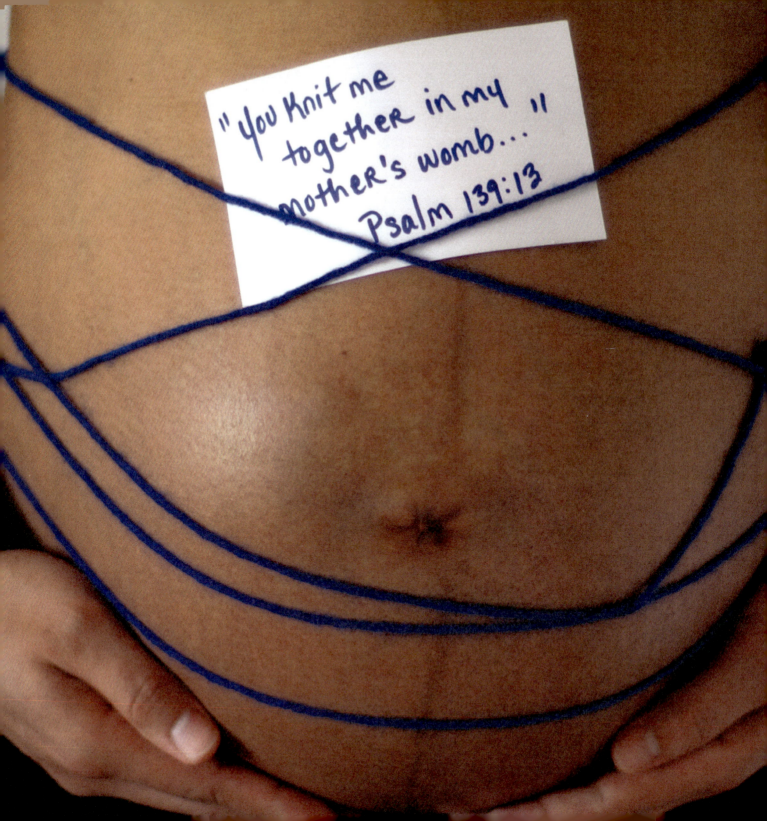

LUKE 2:40

"There the child grew up healthy and strong. He was filled with wisdom, and God's favor was on him." Lord God, I pray that your favor and blessing will DWELL all throughout and encompass my child's life. God I pray that my baby grows healthy and stronger physically, mentally, emotionally. I pray that every fiber of their being is functioning PROPERLY and EFFECTIVELY. I pray that anything that contradicts my child's optimal HEALTH is cast down right now in Jesus' name. I pray that my child learns to care for their body so that they can effectively serve you. I pray asking that you BLESS my child with a LONG LIFE full of PROSPERITY in their MIND, BODY and SPIRIT. Father God, I pray that my child will find favor wherever they go. I thank you Father that my child will seek you in all situations for your WISDOM and that their WISE decisions will please you and have a positive effect on your people and your kingdom. I pray that my child will open their heart to the leading and guiding of the HOLY SPIRIT and will accept JESUS as their SAVIOR.

PROVERBS 22:6

"Direct your children onto the right path, and when they are older, they will not leave it." God, I declare in Jesus' name that your Word will be the FOUNDATION and CENTER of my child's life. God, I pray that my child knows YOUR VOICE and LISTENS for your direction daily and TRUSTS what they will learn from YOUR WORD. I believe God, that the SEEDS of your love will DIRECT and INFLUENCE every decision and choice that my child makes in all situations. I pray that my child is PROTECTED from negative influences and is SMART and WISE enough to keep their eyes FOCUSED ON YOU. God, I pray that my child has a heart that wants to do good and wants to LIVE RIGHT. I pray that my child will be strong when faced with temptation to live outside of your will and YOUR BEST. I pray God that my child's love for your Word will inspire others to choose you and accept Jesus as Savior. Father God, I ask for the GRACE necessary to teach my child about your Word. I declare that my child will CARRY YOUR PROMISES in their heart FOREVER.

PSALM 138:8

"The lord will work out his plans for my life for your faithful love, o Lord endures forever. Don't abandon me, for you made me." Father God, I pray that my child will fulfill your will and purpose for their life. REVEAL to my baby's heart all that you've called them to do. I pray FOCUS, DISCIPLINE, WILLINGNESS, PASSION and AMBITION over my child's MIND, WILL and EMOTIONS. I declare that in all situations, my child will consider YOUR LOVE and allow that love to GUIDE them throughout life. I pray that my baby will grow to stay TRUE to Jesus and will follow JESUS' EXAMPLE daily. I ask God that you go ahead of my child and work out your plans for their life. Make a way out of no way God when they need it. STRAIGHTEN their path God when they are straying. God, I pray that nothing will deter my child from fulfilling your plan for their life. I REBUKE the enemy's plan to distract or destroy my child's focus on you. I thank you Father, that your love will never leave my child and that because they REMAIN FOCUSED on YOU, they will experience your BEST!

I TIMOTHY 4:12

"Don't let anyone think less of you because you are young. Be an example to all believers in what you say, in the way you live, in your love, your faith, and your purity." God, I thank you that my child is ANOINTED with a heart that wants to FOLLOW JESUS, is concerned about PLEASING YOU and is proud to be CHOSEN by you to fulfill your will. I pray that my baby will be a LEADER for you God. Father, I declare over my child that they will be an example to others in life and FAITH. I believe and declare that the purpose you have for my child will INSPIRE and influence others to CHOOSE CHRIST. I pray that my child takes on your VOICE in this world. I declare in Jesus' name that my child is WISE and SPIRITUALLY MATURING as they focus and MEDITATE on your Word. I pray that my child answers the call you have for their life according to your appointed time and season. I thank you Father God that all situations are working out for their good and are in line with YOUR PURPOSE for their life.

EPHESIANS 2:10

"For we are God's masterpiece. He has created us anew in Christ Jesus, so we can do the good things he planned for us long ago." Lord God, I pray that my baby grows to know how **SPECIAL** and important they are to you and your plan. I pray God that my child knows that they are an amazing **MASTERPIECE, RELEVANT** and **NEEDED**. I pray that you help my child develop a **STRONG SELF-ESTEEM** and **SELF-RESPECT** that is **ROOTED** in the realization that they are **UNIQUELY CREATED** by you, with an amazing purpose. God, I pray that my child **CHERISHES** their **UNIQUENESS** and openly displays it for your glory. I pray God that my baby will feel **CONFIDENT** because they know in their heart that you created them in **YOUR IMAGE**. I pray that my child knows that there is no comparison to the talent and gifts you've given them. I pray that my child has **HEALTHY SELF-LOVE**. I pray Father God that my child will only look to Jesus as the source of their **IDENTITY** and when they need **REASSURANCE**, your Word will confirm their permanent place in your kingdom.

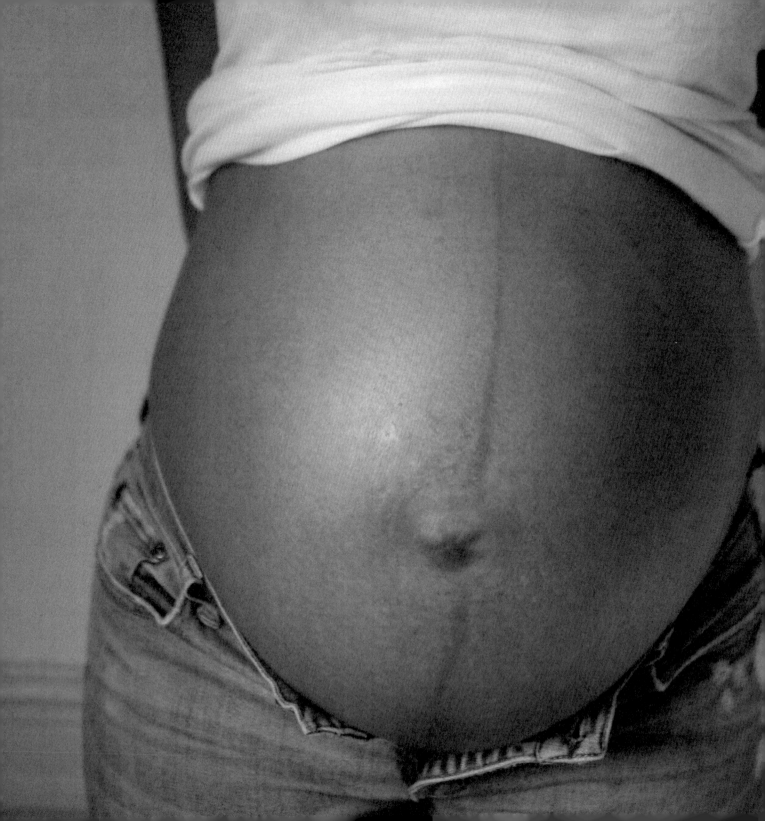

PSALM 119:33

"Direct my footsteps according to your word; let no sin rule over me." Father God, I pray that my child always looks to your Word for wisdom, purpose and your will for their life journey. I pray that your Word is my baby's guiding light and only SOURCE OF TRUTH. God, I pray that my baby has a HEART that follows you their ENTIRE LIFE. I declare in Jesus' name that they have an overwhelming desire to always be in YOUR PRESENCE. God I pray that my child only follows you. I pray Father that my child will always seek you for DIRECTION and GUIDANCE. I pray that my child learns your Word and holds your PROMISES dear so that when they are faced with challenges and temptations, they CLING to you and are STRENGTHENED where they are weak. I pray God that my child is MOTIVATED to please you by following your instruction for their life. I pray that my child wants to HONOR. God I pray that your Word becomes a SHIELD around my baby's HEART; defending every fiber of their unique being from anything that contradicts YOUR BEST.

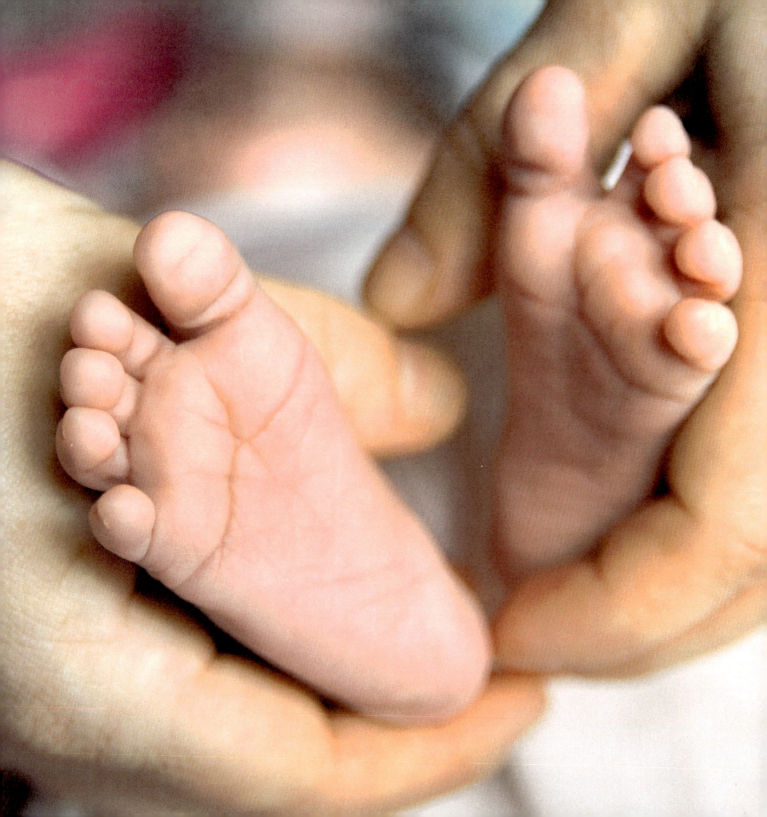

Made in the USA
Columbia, SC
04 August 2017